WASH
YOUR HANDS

Vicky Bureau

A Crabtree Roots Plus Book

Crabtree Publishing
crabtreebooks.com

School-to-Home Support for Caregivers and Teachers

This book helps children grow by letting them practice reading. Here are a few guiding questions to help the reader with building his or her comprehension skills. Possible answers appear here in red.

Before Reading:
- What do I think this book is about?
    - *I think this book is about why I need to wash my hands.*
    - *I think this book is about when and how to wash my hands.*
- What do I want to learn about this topic?
    - *I want to learn about keeping my hands clean.*
    - *I want to learn about tools I can use to keep my hands clean.*

During Reading:
- I wonder why…
    - *I wonder why washing my hands keeps them clean.*
    - *I wonder how I can keep germs away from my hands.*
- What have I learned so far?
    - *I have learned that clean hands are a healthy habit.*
    - *I have learned that germs can live on hands.*

After Reading:
- What details did I learn about this topic?
    - *I have learned how to wash my hands.*
    - *I have learned that soap helps to clean my hands.*
- Read the book again and look for the vocabulary words.
    - *I see the word **germs** on page 8 and the word **lather** on page 13. The other vocabulary words are found on page 23.*

Clean hands are a healthy **habit**.

A healthy habit is something you do to stay well.

Hands touch many things.

Fingers touch many things.

Germs can live on hands.

Germs can make us sick.

Washing your hands is easy.

All you need is soap and water.

Soap helps to clean your hands.

Water makes a bubbly **lather**.

Scrub in between your fingers.

Scrub underneath your nails.

Next, **rinse** with water.

Then, dry with a clean towel.

That's it!

That's all it takes to have clean hands!

Clean hands keep germs away.

Washing your hands is a healthy habit!

Word List
Sight Words

away	helps	sick
between	keep	soap
bubbly	live	things
easy	make	touch
fingers	many	towel
hands	need	underneath
healthy	next	water

Words to Know

 clean

 germs

 habit

 lather

 rinse

 scrub

WASH YOUR HANDS

Written by: Vicky Bureau
Designed by: Kathy Walsh
Series Development: James Earley
Proofreader: Melissa Boyce
Educational Consultant: Marie Lemke M.Ed.

Photographs:
Shutterstock: Cover: ucchie79 Mochipet; pg 3 & 23 MIA Studio; pg 4 Sergey Novikov; pg 6 Matt Jeppson; pg 7 Pixavril; pg 8 & 23 SweetLeMontea; pg 9 Bernardo Emanuelle; pg 10 Luis Molinero; p 11 Gyorgy Barna, MidoSemsem; pg 12 & 23 LooksLikeLisa; pg 13 & 23 3445128471; pg 14, 15 & 23 Regreto; pg 16 myboys.me; pg 17 PeopleImages.com - Yuri A; pg 18 SKT Studio; pg 19 NYS; pg 20 Oksana Kuzmina; pg 21 Hogan Imaging

Crabtree Publishing

crabtreebooks.com   800.387.7650
Copyright © 2024 Crabtree Publishing

All rights reserved. No part of this publication may be reproduced, stored in a retrieval system or be transmitted in any form or by any means, electronic, mechanical, photocopying, recording, or otherwise, without the prior written permission of Crabtree Publishing.

Printed in the U.S.A./072023/CG20230214

Published in Canada
Crabtree Publishing
616 Welland Ave
St. Catharines, Ontario
L2M 5V6

Published in the United States
Crabtree Publishing
347 Fifth Ave
Suite 1402-145
New York, NY 10016

Library and Archives Canada Cataloguing in Publication
Available at Library and Archives Canada

Library of Congress Cataloging-in-Publication Data
Available at the Library of Congress

Hardcover: 978-1-0398-0985-7
Paperback: 978-1-0398-1038-9
Ebook (pdf): 978-1-0398-1144-7
Epub: 978-1-0398-1091-4